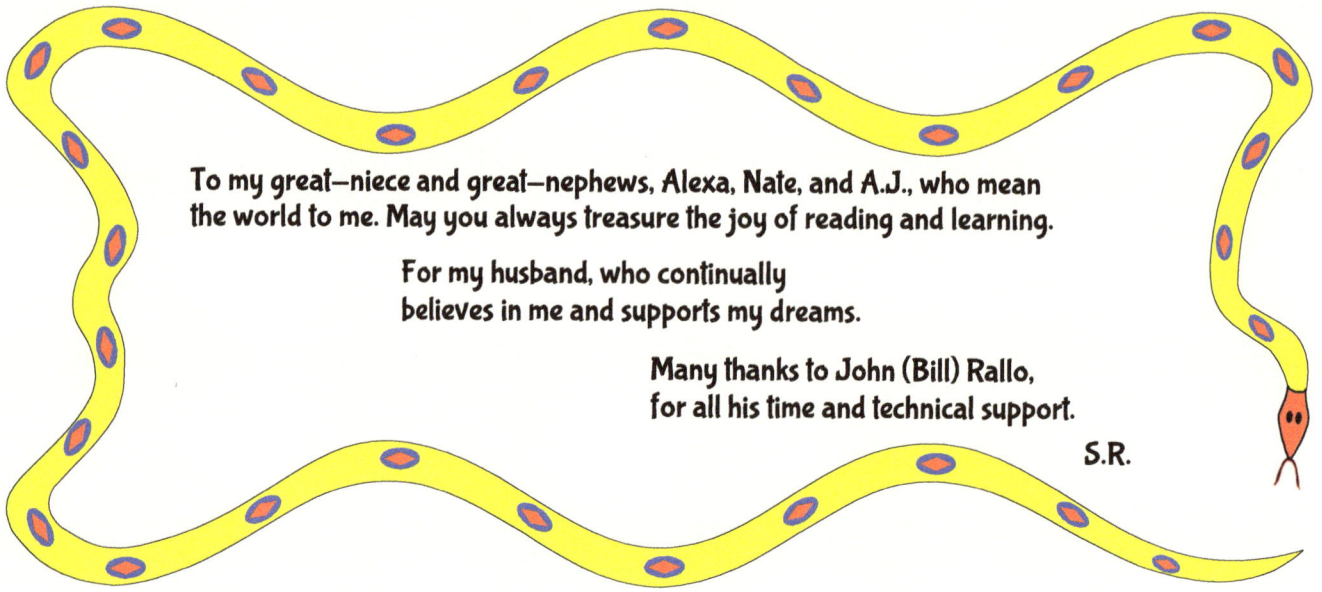

To my great–niece and great–nephews, Alexa, Nate, and A.J., who mean the world to me. May you always treasure the joy of reading and learning.

For my husband, who continually believes in me and supports my dreams.

Many thanks to John (Bill) Rallo, for all his time and technical support.

S.R.

ISBN: 978-1-7335015-4-5 (hardcover)
ISBN: 978-1-7335015-3-8 (paperback)
ISBN: 978-1-7335015-5-2 (e-book)

Library of Congress Control Number: 2021909521

Some animals have gross eating habits, involving blood, butts, and barf. Find out the absolutely dreadful things some creatures eat and the nasty ways some animals get their food.

Subjects: 1. Animals-Nonfiction 2. Animal Behavior-Nonfiction 3. Eating Habits-Nonfiction 4. Science-Nonfiction 5. Adaptation-Nonfiction

Printed in the United States of America

Published by Tailgator Press

Email: tailgatorpress@gmail.com

For information about Tailgator Press or this author visit tailgatorpress.com

The Paper Heart, the author's first book, is available on Amazon.

WE'RE GROSS BUTT, WE CAN'T HELP IT!

(YUCKY STUFF ANIMALS LOVE TO EAT)

by Sally Reichert

TAILGATOR PRESS

TABLE OF CONTENTS

ALL THE UNDERLINED WORDS IN THIS BOOK ARE ALSO IN THE GLOSSARY.

Freaky Frogs

HAVE YOU EVER THOUGHT ABOUT MAKING YOUR HOME IN A HUGE,
SMELLY MOUND OF ELEPHANT POOP? PROBABLY NOT, BUT ELEPHANT
POOP, AS IT TURNS OUT, MAKES A GREAT HOME SO LONG AS YOU
CAN HANDLE THE STINK. JUST ASK THE ORNATE NARROW-MOUTHED FROG.

5

Hi. You'll usually find me partly buried
in leaf litter on the forest floor. But what do I do during dry
season when there are not enough leaves on the ground?
I hang out in elephant <u>dung</u>, of course!
Elephant <u>dung</u>, or poop, is cooler and more humid
than air. Plus, there are leftover hunks of food to
eat that the elephant didn't digest.
The many bugs living in the elephant <u>dung</u>, such as beetles,
ants, spiders, termites, and crickets, also make
it a tasty treat.

ornate narrow-mouthed frog

It's bad enough I live
in elephant poop, but what was
I thinking when I picked such a
large animal, since I'm only
one inch (2.5 centimeters) long?

6

7 CONTINENTS

NORTH AMERICA

EUROPE

ASIA

AFRICA

SOUTH AMERICA

AUSTRALIA

ANTARCTICA

N W E S

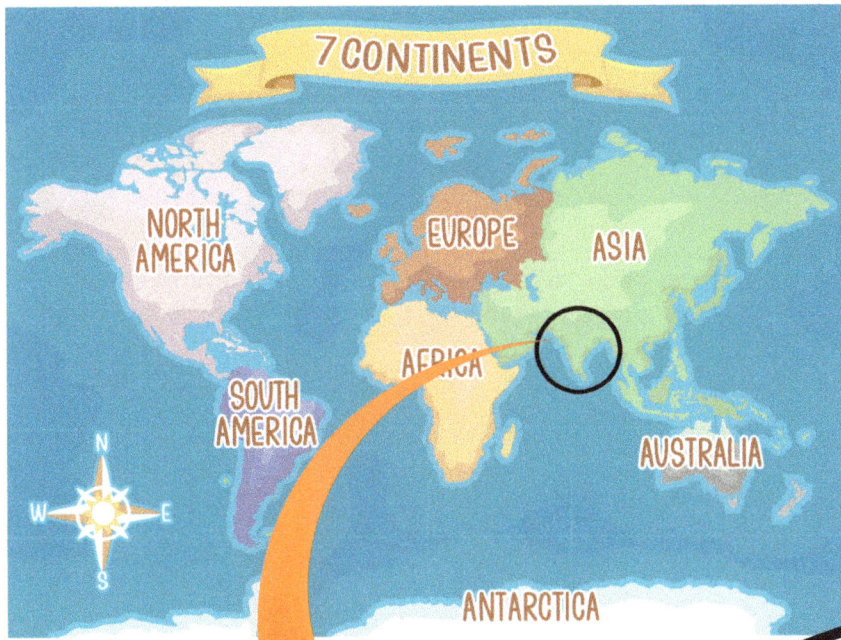

Where do I live?

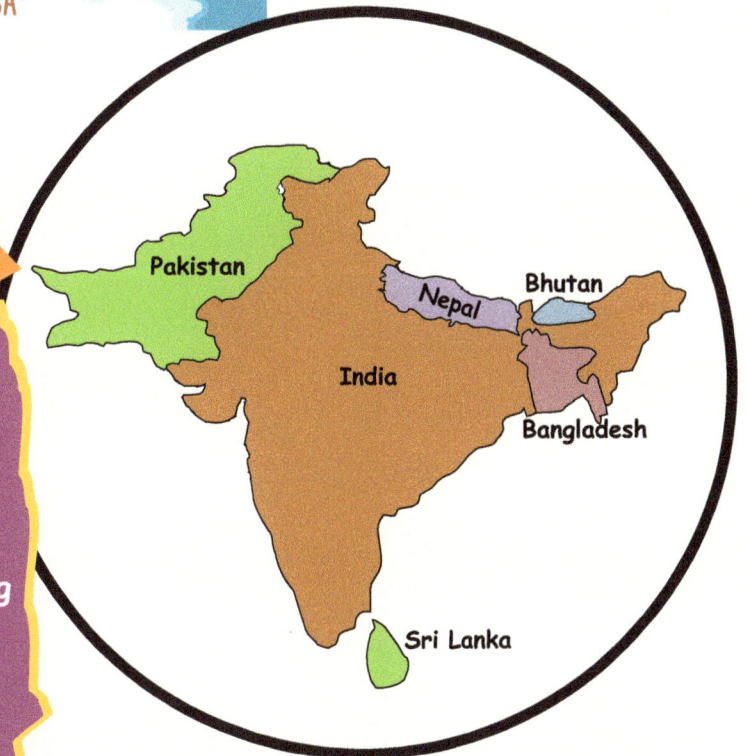

Pakistan

Nepal

Bhutan

India

Bangladesh

Sri Lanka

DID YOU KNOW?

- The ornate narrow-mouthed frog is found in Bangladesh, Bhutan, India, Nepal, Pakistan, and Sri Lanka.

- The ornate narrow-mouthed frog weighs less than a paper clip.

- These frogs are poor swimmers, but excellent hoppers.

- Females are slightly larger than males.

- The frog is nocturnal, although during the rainy season it is lively in the daytime, too.

- The ornate narrow-mouthed frog lives 5 years at the most.

7

I'M GROSS, BUT I CAN'T HELP IT. I'M A FILTHY ANIMAL!

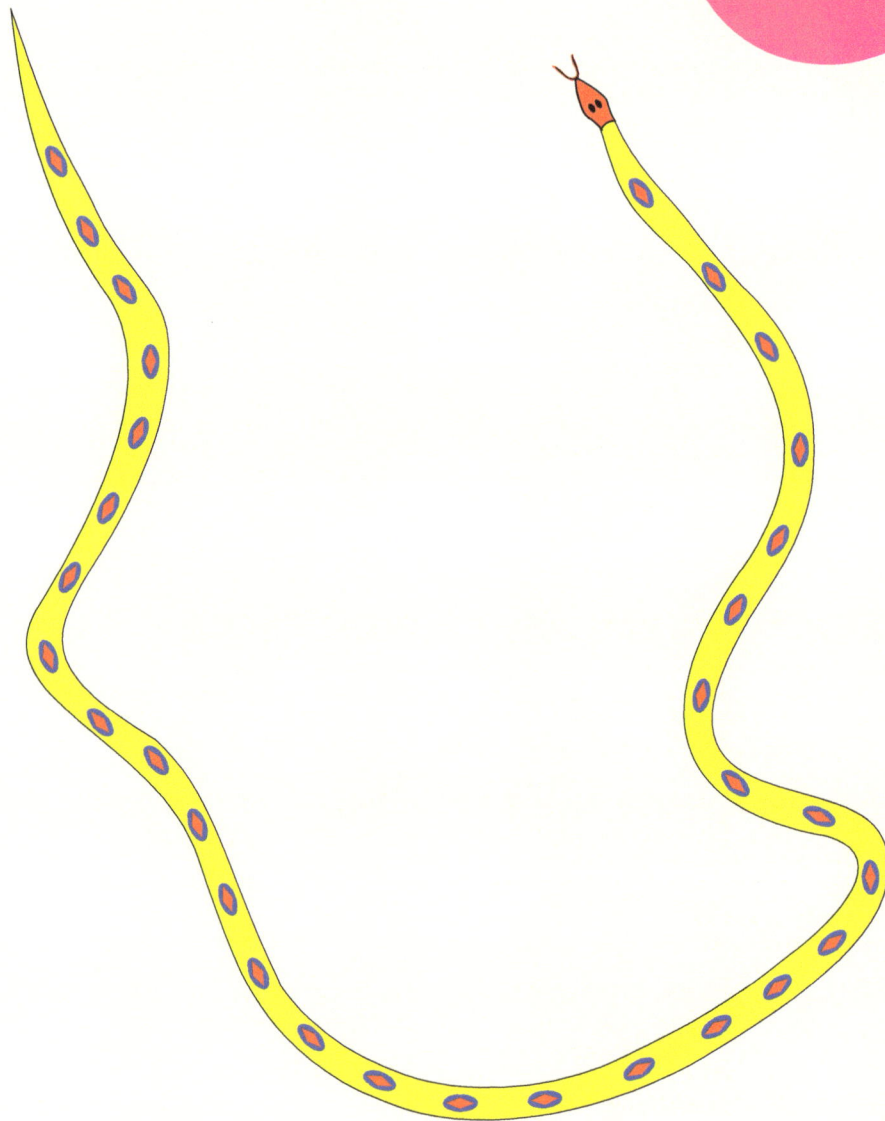

8

Pukey Pups

VOMIT IS A FANCY WORD FOR PUKE OR THROWING UP. YUK! HAVE YOU EVER HAD A CLASSMATE PUKE IN CLASS, OR YOU HAD TO STEP OVER IT IN THE HALLWAY AT SCHOOL? THAT'S ENOUGH TO MAKE SOMEONE ELSE THROW UP, BUT THAT WOULD BE A FEAST IF YOU WERE A WOLF PUP. WOLF PUPS ARE TOO ADORABLE TO BE DISGUSTING. HOWEVER, WOLVES ARE WELL-KNOWN FOR THROWING UP FOOD FOR THEIR BABIES. AS CRAZY AS IT SOUNDS, WOLF PUPS LOVE IT!

Vomit. Yum! After three weeks of only drinking milk, I need meat! I'm too little to hunt on my own, so I'm lucky my parents hunt and share their food with me. The easiest way for my mom and dad to bring me food is in their stomach since they don't have hands.

I follow my mom and dad around, and when I'm hungry, I lick their mouths. This causes them to throw up what they just ate into my mouth. This might sound terrible to you, but I think it's delicious!

Come closer. I have one more silly thing to tell you. Because I'm a new pup, my mom has to massage my belly with her warm tongue in order for me to go to the bathroom. Shhh! Don't tell anyone.

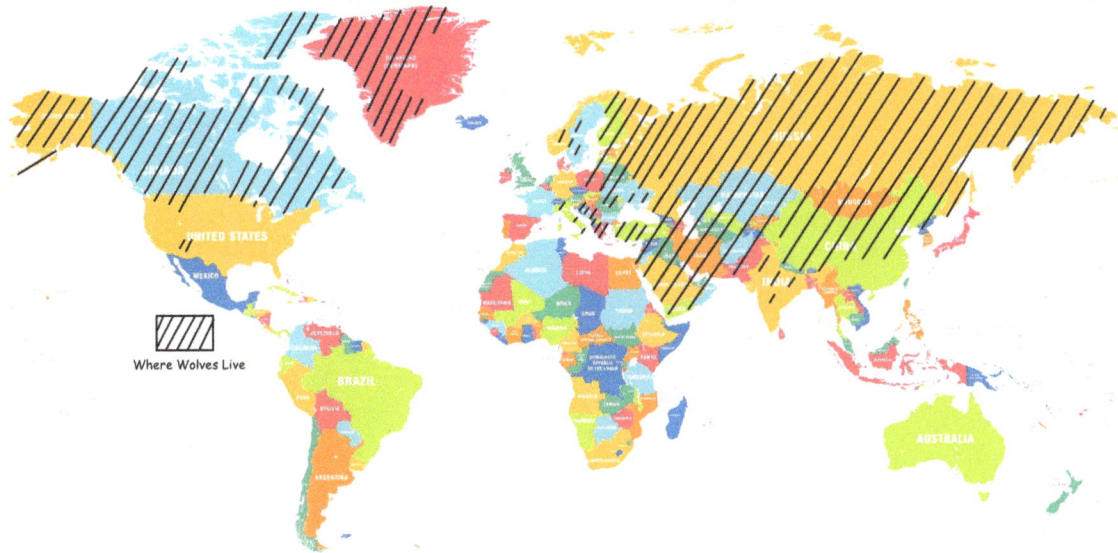

Where Wolves Live

Where do I live?

DID YOU KNOW?

- **Regurgitate** - means to throw up
- Pups are born blind and deaf.
- At birth, pups weigh only one pound. That's about the weight of a bag of rice.
- After birth, pups don't open their eyes for fifteen days.
- Wolves live in family groups called packs.
- Wolves can swim up to 8 miles.
- Wolves run on their toes, which helps them to stop and turn quickly.
- Many birds also **regurgitate** to feed their babies.

Wolf Pups Eating

WE'RE GROSS, BUT WE CAN'T HELP IT. WE'RE FILTHY ANIMALS!

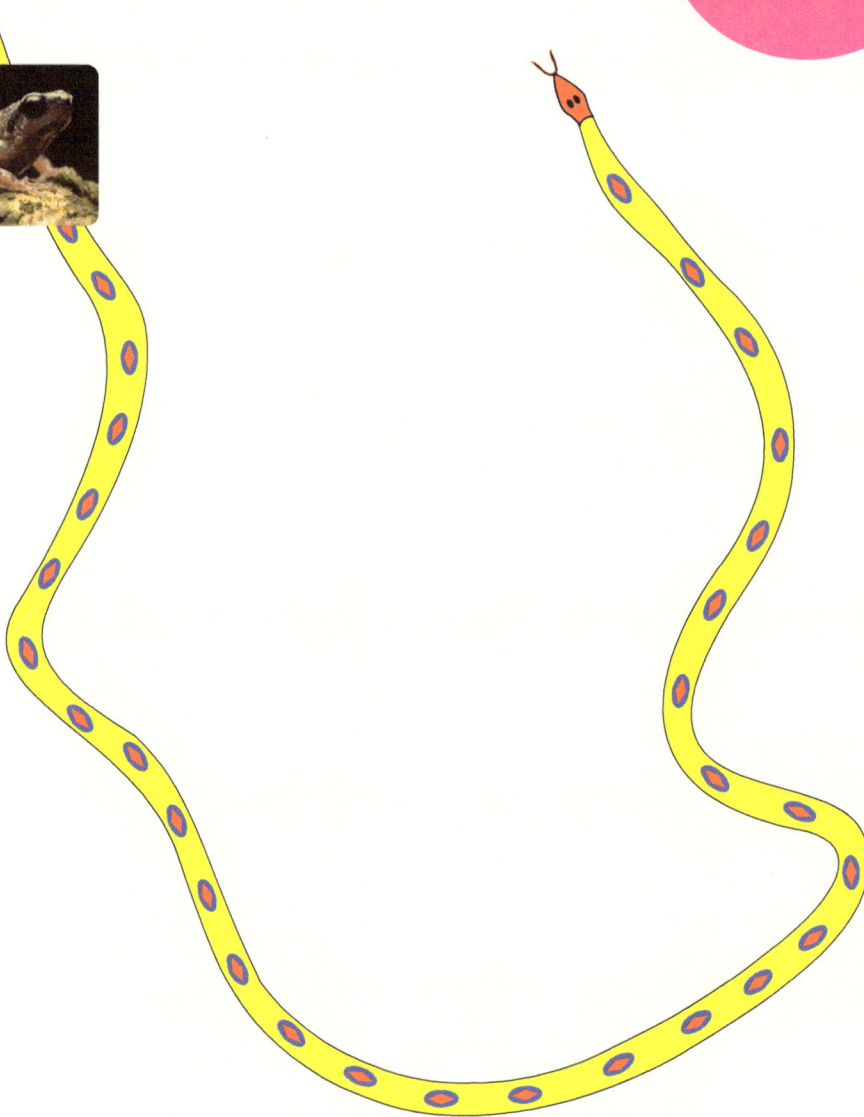

SLURPY SLUDGE

WOLF PUPS AREN'T THE ONLY ANIMALS THAT USE VOMIT TO EAT.
THOSE PESKY HOUSEFLIES ALSO USE VOMIT. THEIR OWN! THE
HOUSEFLY HAS A MOUTHPART THAT'S LIKE A STRAW USED TO
SIP OR SOAK UP FOOD, BUT WAIT UNTIL YOU HEAR HOW THEY
PREPARE THEIR FOOD FOR EATING!

Hi. It's me. The annoying housefly that loves to bother you while you're trying to eat. I love landing on your food and then you try to swat me, but I'm too quick. I don't have teeth for chewing, so I can't just grab the food and fly away. I need to sit for a minute first. Want to know why? You don't want to be eating while I explain this or you'll be sorry!

I don't have teeth, but I like to gobble foods like your steak or pizza. Guess what I do? I sit on your food and vomit and then wait a minute. It's like adding hot water to oatmeal. My vomit causes the food to break up into soft pieces. Then I use my proboscis (like a straw) and suck it up. You kind of do the same thing. When you chew food, it mixes with saliva in your mouth and softens it.

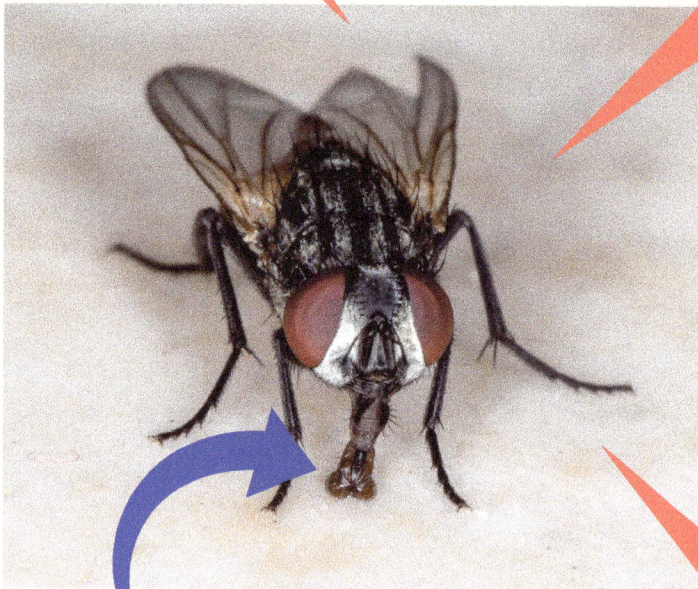

proboscis

If you think I'm disgusting, listen to this. I love to land on and eat nasty things, like feces (poop) and rotting food. That nasty stuff clings to my legs. When I walk on your sandwich, all that nasty stuff gets on your food. Yuk!

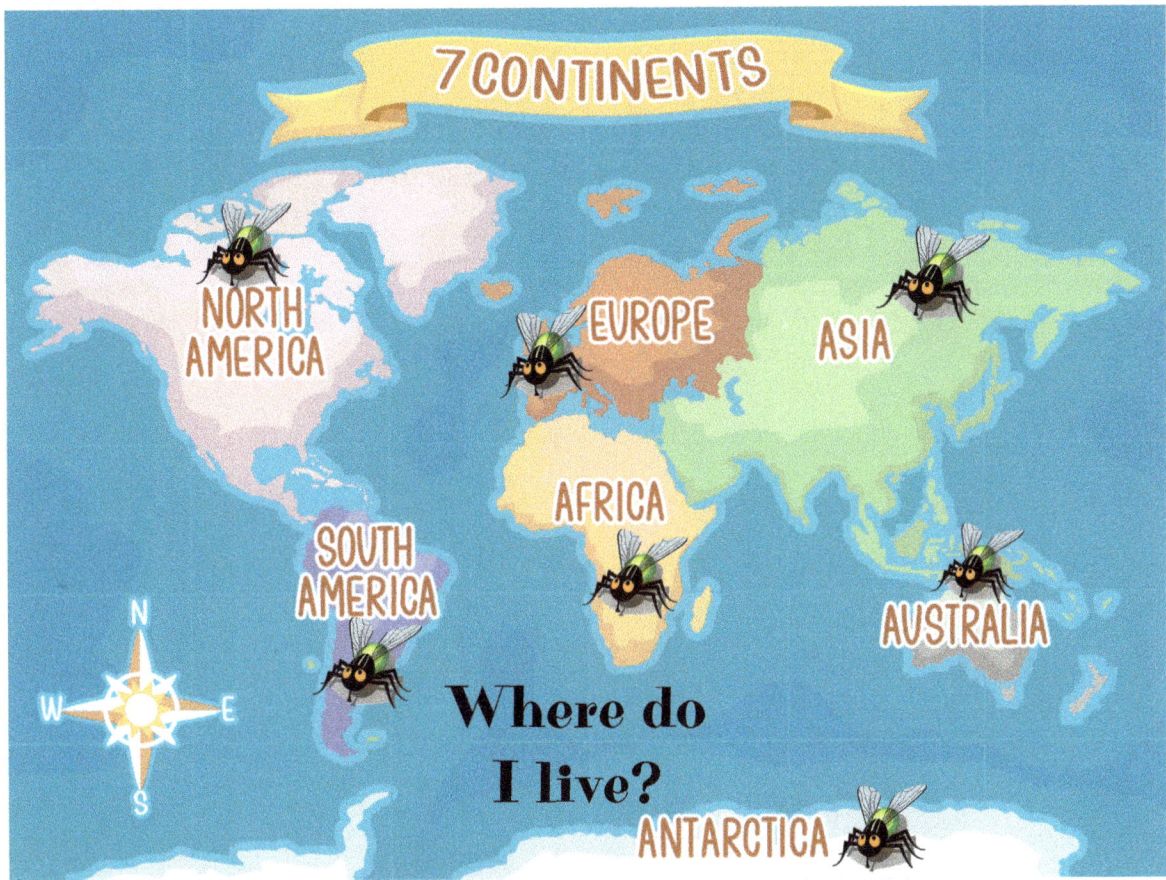

7 CONTINENTS

NORTH AMERICA

EUROPE

ASIA

AFRICA

SOUTH AMERICA

AUSTRALIA

N
W E
S

Where do I live?

ANTARCTICA

DID YOU KNOW?

- Proboscis - A long tube on the outside of the mouth of some insects that is used for sucking. It is spongy.

- Houseflies are one of the most common insects on the planet.

- Flies can spread over 65 diseases to humans.

- Houseflies do not live beyond one month.

- A housefly goes to the bathroom 300 times a day. That's once every 4-5 minutes.

- The housefly is about 1/4 inch (6 to 7 millimeters) long, with the female usually larger than the male.

WE'RE GROSS, BUT WE CAN'T HELP IT. WE'RE FILTHY ANIMALS!

YUMMY MUMMY

HOW MANY TIMES HAVE YOU SAID, "HEY MOM, WHAT'S FOR DINNER?" YOU MIGHT HEAR HER SAY SOMETHING LIKE PIZZA, CHICKEN, MAYBE EVEN SPAGHETTI, BUT WHAT IF SHE SAID YOU WERE HAVING HER FOR DINNER? IF YOU WERE A BLACK LACE-WEAVER SPIDER, YOU WOULD BE EXCITED BECAUSE THAT'S EXACTLY WHAT BLACK LACE-WEAVER SPIDERS EAT. THEIR MOM.

Yummy! Mummy!
I'm having Mom for dinner
and so are my brothers and sisters.
This is our favorite meal because it makes us
strong and helps us live longer. Plus,
if we eat our mom, we won't eat each other
and will continue the family name.

How does this happen?
A day after I'm born,
my mom lays another cluster
of eggs. These eggs are only for
food for my brothers, sisters,
and me. It takes about
three days to eat the eggs.

After that, we still need
to eat, so here's the unusual part.
Our mom begins to shake and vibrate
our web. This tells us that it is
time to eat her. We swarm over
her and suck on her insides like a
milkshake. We release poison
into our mom's body, and she
dies quickly. Eating our mom
is called matriphagy.

By the way, I have
60-130 brothers and sisters.
That's how many eggs my mom
lays. Good thing my mom doesn't
have to name all of us.

18

Where do I live?

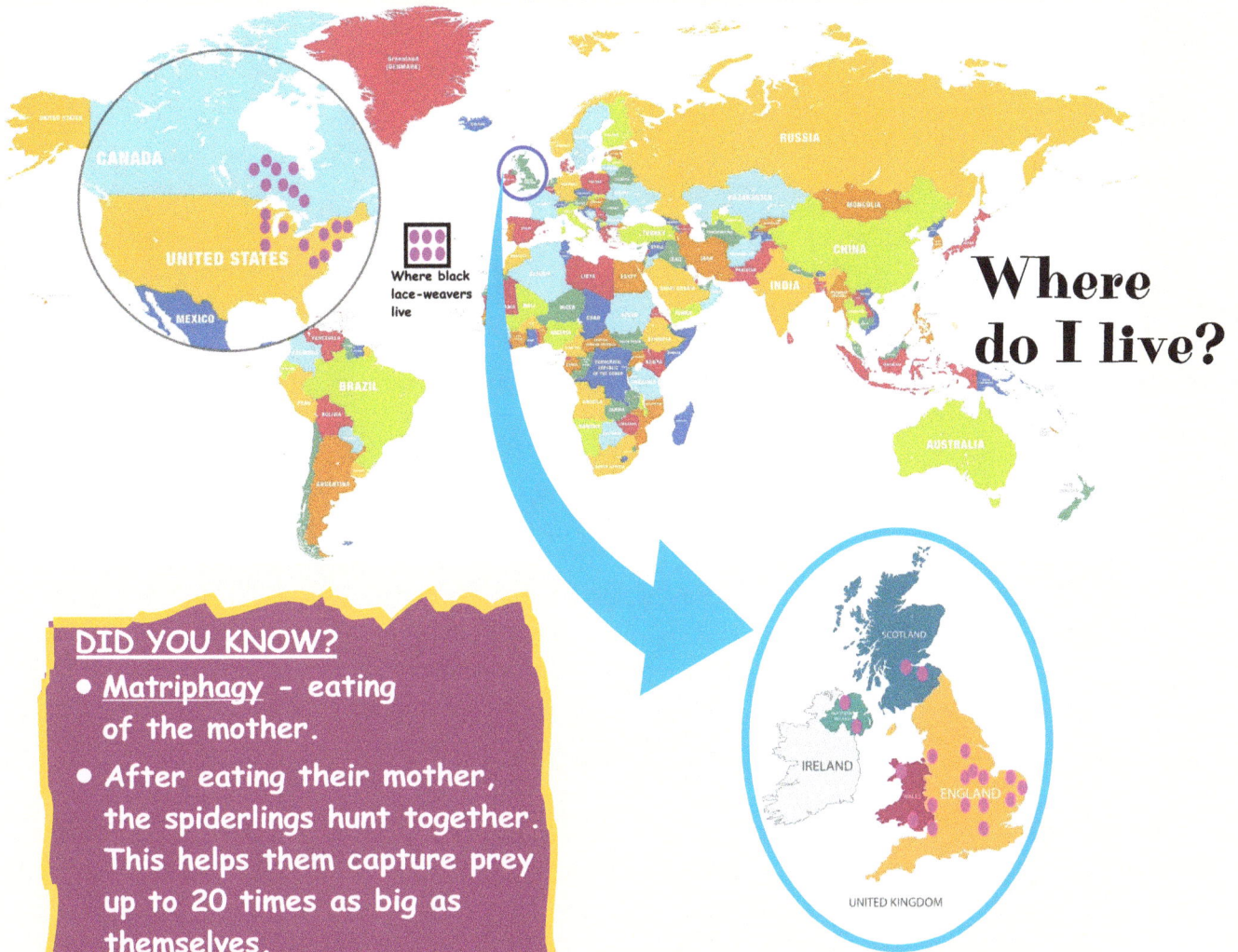

Where black lace-weavers live

DID YOU KNOW?

- <u>Matriphagy</u> - eating of the mother.

- After eating their mother, the spiderlings hunt together. This helps them capture prey up to 20 times as big as themselves.

- The spiderlings live together for one month after eating their mother.

- Black lace-weavers have 8 legs and 8 eyes.

- Black lace-weavers are $\frac{1}{2}$ inch (13 millimeters) long.

- Black lace-weaver spiders' main colors are black, brown, and tan.

- They are usually found under logs, rocks, and gardens.

Egg sac from a black lace-weaver spider containing 60 - 130 spiderlings.

19

WE'RE GROSS, BUT
WE CAN'T HELP IT.
WE'RE FILTHY ANIMALS!

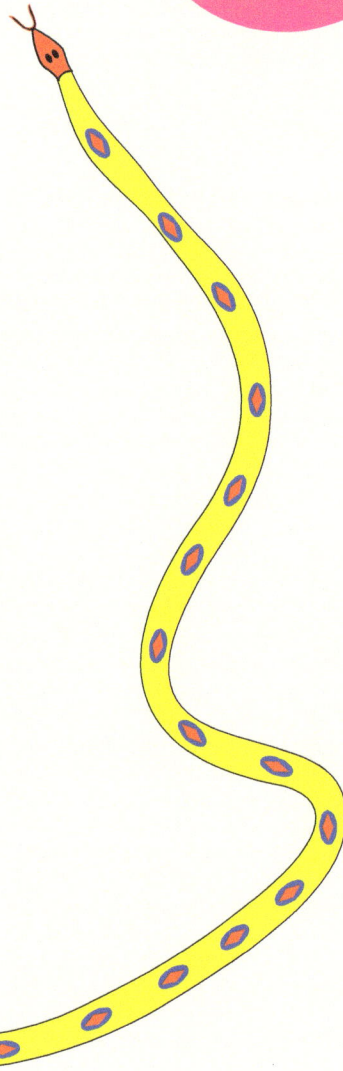

SKIN SPLITTERS

WHAT IF YOU HAD TO EAT THE SAME THING FOR DINNER EVERY DAY? WOULD YOU GET TIRED OF IT? CAECILIAN BABIES LOVE EATING THE SAME THING OVER AND OVER AND OVER. BELIEVE IT OR NOT, THEY EAT THEIR MOTHER'S SKIN. UNLIKE THE BLACK LACE-WEAVER SPIDER, CAECILIAN BABIES ARE A LITTLE NICER AND DON'T KILL THEIR MOTHER. IF THEY DID, THEY WOULD RUN OUT OF FOOD.

21

Hi. I'm a Taita African caecilian. As my name says, I make my home in Kenya, Africa. When I'm a baby, I do the craziest thing. I eat my mother's skin, and it is quite appetizing.

I have fangs that help me strip the skin off my mother, which is full of nutrients. Then, in a few days, she grows another layer that I peel off and eat. There is a fancy word for eating her skin – dermatotrophy.

This does not hurt my mom. Once I'm 3 inches long (80 millimeters), I live on my own and have mouthwatering meals of termites, earthworms, and ants.

We are not seen very much because we live underground. Some people think we are worms or snakes, but we are actually amphibians. There are 200 species of caecilians. We are kind of strange. We have no legs or arms, and since we live underground we have no ears and eyes, although some of us have tiny eyes under our skin.

We can sense vibrations and see light and dark. Tentacles on our face can detect food and help us find our way around. We are strong diggers and make our way through the dirt as easily as a shovel.

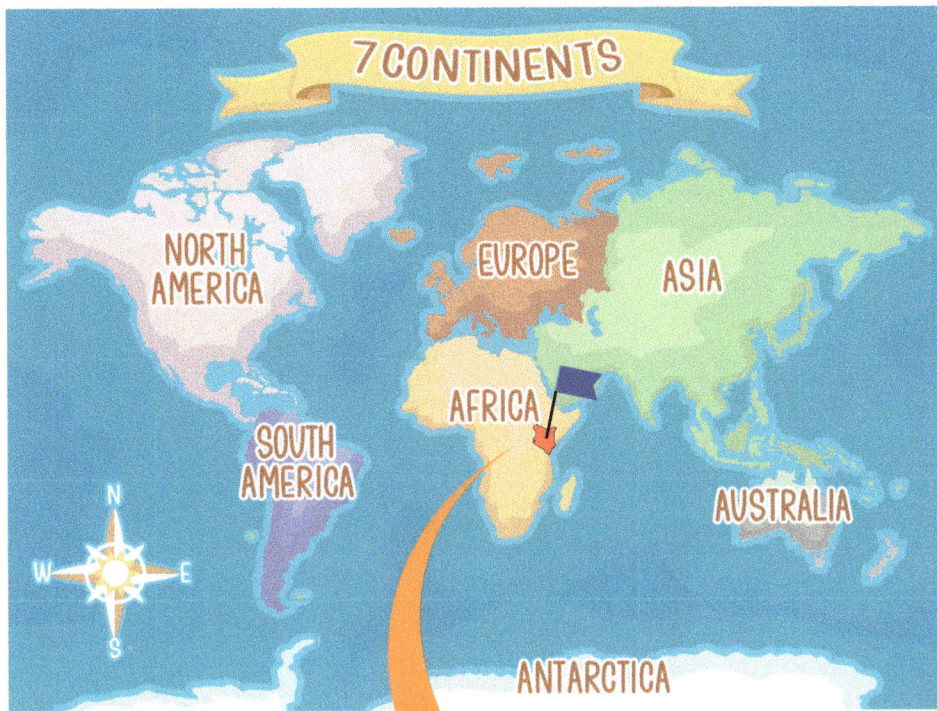

Where do I live?

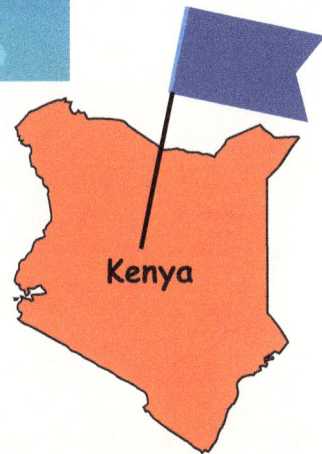

Kenya

- Dermatotrophy - to eat a parent's skin. This is unique to Caecilians.
- Caecilians' skin is smooth and slimy.
- Males reach 13.5 inches (348 millimeters) in length.
- Females reach 13 inches (333 millimeters) in length.
- The largest Caecilian is 5 feet (1.5 meters) found in Colombia in South America.
- The smallest species is 3.5 inches (90 millimeters) found in Cameroon in Africa.

Taita African caecilian

23

WE'RE GROSS, BUT
WE CAN'T HELP IT.
WE'RE FILTHY ANIMALS!

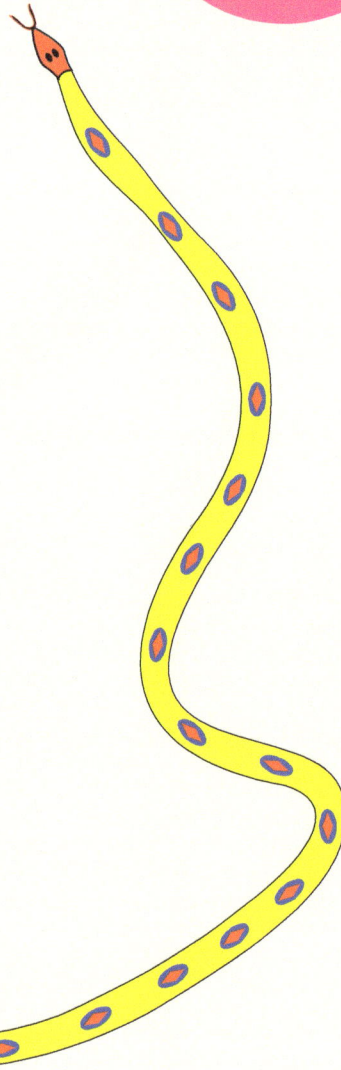

Fierce Finch

HALLOWEEN TIME IS A TIME OF YEAR THAT WE HEAR ABOUT VAMPIRES. MANY CHILDREN DRESS UP AS VAMPIRES FOR THIS DAY. WHEN WE THINK OF VAMPIRES WE THINK OF DEAD HUMANS WHO HAVE COME BACK TO LIFE, WITH LARGE FANGS AND ONLY COME OUT AT NIGHT. THEY ATTACK PEOPLE, HAVE PALE-COLORED SKIN AND RED EYES. DRACULA IS A WELL-KNOWN VAMPIRE. WHAT DOES THIS BIRD HAVE TO DO WITH VAMPIRES? IT'S A VAMPIRE FINCH. DRACULA AND THE VAMPIRE FINCH HAVE ONE THING IN COMMON. THEY BOTH LOVE SUCKING BLOOD.

By looking at me, you would probably never call me a vampire, but that's what I am. I'm a vampire finch, and I love sucking blood from this booby.

I suck blood when other food is in short supply. Get this, sometimes I even drink vomit of other birds.

Are you wondering why I put up with this? Well, there are so many finches on this island that if I fight off one, there's always more around to jump on.

Not only do I suck blood, I also steal boobies' eggs. Even though my beak is sharp, I can't break the shell, so I roll and kick the egg into rocks. This breaks the egg open, and I can then suck up the yellow yolk. My friends want the liquid, too, so sometimes we fight over it.

26

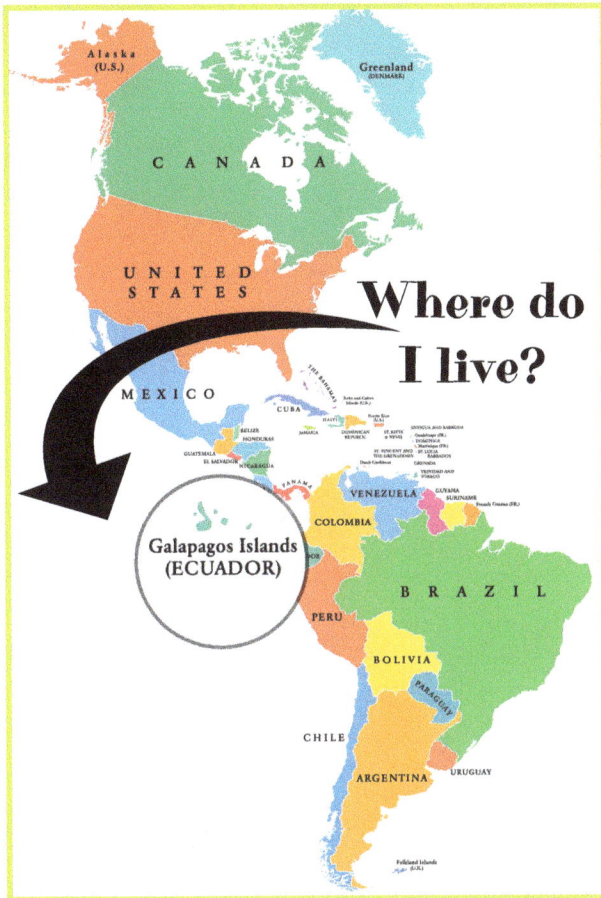

Where do I live?

Galapagos Islands (ECUADOR)

DID YOU KNOW?

- Vampire finches live only on the Galapagos Islands.

- They live 5 – 10 years.

- Vampire finches weigh less than an ounce (28 grams). That's less than the weight of a slice of bread.

- The female finch lays 3 eggs.

- Baby finches can fly after two weeks.

- The finch's beak color varies from black to orange, depending on the season.

WE'RE GROSS, BUT WE CAN'T HELP IT. WE'RE FILTHY ANIMALS!

28

Squishy Grapes

WOULDN'T YOU LOVE THIS ADORABLE RABBIT FOR A PET? ISN'T IT SO
CUTE? WELL, WHAT YOU'RE ABOUT TO FIND OUT MAY NOT SEEM SO CUTE
AND ADORABLE. JUST LIKE YOU, RABBITS NEED TO EAT HEALTHY SO THEY
CAN GET THE VITAMINS AND NUTRITION THEY NEED TO GROW AND LIVE TO
BE OLD. RABBITS EAT GRASS AND WEEDS, BUT WAIT. THIS ADORABLE
CREATURE HAS ANOTHER WAY OF STAYING HEALTHY-BY EATING ITS OWN
POOP. YES, YOU HEARD ME RIGHT.

Hey!! I'm not the only animal that eats poop. In fact, baby elephants eat their mother's poop. Yuk! Seriously, I have to eat my poop in order to be healthy. Basically, I eat, then poop, then eat it again. Eating my own poop is called <u>Coprophagy</u>.

I'm an herbivore, which means I eat grass and weeds. Some plants are hard to break down in my gut, so I don't absorb as many vitamins as I need.

When I eat, food is digested and I poop out round pellets like Coco Puffs. Some of the food stays in a special place in my gut longer to make it softer like a bunch of grapes. These are called <u>cecotropes</u>.

The so-called grapes contain a lot of nutrition, so when I poop that out, I eat it so I can take in all the vitamins and nutrients I didn't get the first time I ate.

I usually eat my poop when you are not looking. I'm pretty polite. If I didn't eat my poop, I would starve and die, so my owner should never try to stop me.

rabbit

By the way, why does everyone want to call me a hare and call hares rabbits? We're different!

hare

Rabbits' ears are short and hares' ears are longer.

Baby rabbits are born blind with no fur. Baby hares can see at birth and have fur.

Rabbits like to live more under-ground and hares like to live above ground.

Rabbits make good pets because they can be tamed. Hares can't. They stay wild.

Rabbit fur never changes color. Hares' fur changes color from summer to winter.

Rabbits are more social than hares.

DID YOU KNOW?
- Feces - poop
- The squishy poop (cecotropes) is very stinky.
- Like dogs, rabbits can be trained to sit in your lap, do tricks, and come when their name is called.
- Rabbits' teeth never stop growing.
- Bunnies cannot vomit.
- Pet rabbits live 8-12 years. Wild rabbits live 1-2 years.
- A herd is a group of rabbits.

WE'RE GROSS, BUT
WE CAN'T HELP IT.
WE'RE FILTHY ANIMALS!

Tasty Tears

AHH, BUTTERFLIES...BRING JOY AND HAPPINESS. THEY ARE RELAXING TO WATCH. THEY ARE BEAUTIFUL CREATURES WITH SOME OF THE MOST STRIKING COLORS FOUND IN NATURE. KIDS LOVE TO CHASE BUTTERFLIES AND CATCH THEM WITH NETS, AND THEN LET THEM GO. WELL, NOT TO BURST YOUR BUBBLE, BUT THERE'S MORE TO BUTTERFLIES THAN MEETS THE EYE. HOLD TIGHT AND YOU'LL SOON FIND OUT SOMETHING UNUSUAL THAT THEY DO TO SURVIVE.

I can't believe someone is writing about me in a book. I'm nervous. I feel like I have butterflies in my stomach. (That's an idiom.) Oh wait, I am a butterfly. Well, I'm still nervous. Yup, that's me on the turtle's eye. I live in the Amazon and drink the tears of turtles.

I'm not able to get enough sodium (salt) from flowers, so I use my _proboscis_, just like the housefly, to suck up tears from turtles. The tears contain minerals I need.

You won't believe where butterflies who don't live near the Amazon River get their sodium...from poop and dirt.

yellow-spotted river turtle

34

Where do I live?

DID YOU KNOW?

- <u>Lachryphagy</u> - feeding on tears
- These butterflies are called Julia butterflies.
- Male Julia butterflies are a brighter orange color than the females.
- The yellow-spotted river turtle is one of the largest South American river turtles. It weighs 17 pounds (8 kilograms).
- Butterflies can taste with their feet.
- Julia butterflies can also be found in the southern United States, Central America, and the Caribbean.
- The Amazon River is 4,000 miles (6,400 kilometers) long. This is the distance from New York City to Rome, Italy.
- The Amazon River drains into the Atlantic Ocean.

WE'RE GROSS, BUT
WE CAN'T HELP IT.
WE'RE FILTHY ANIMALS!

Young Blood

YIKES! WHAT IS THIS? IT LOOKS LIKE SOMETHING FROM A SPOOKY MOVIE. YOU WOULDN'T WANT TO RUN INTO IT ON THE STREET AT NIGHT. ALTHOUGH YOU REALLY DON'T HAVE TO WORRY ABOUT THAT, BECAUSE EVEN THOUGH IT DOESN'T LOOK LIKE IT, THIS CREATURE IS ACTUALLY VERY SMALL. IT IS AN ANT, BUT NOT JUST ANY ANT. YOU'VE ALREADY HEARD ABOUT THE VAMPIRE FINCH, SO IT ONLY SEEMS FITTING TO INTRODUCE YOU TO THE DRACULA ANT. YES, THIS IS TRULY THE NAME OF AN ANT. JUST LIKE THE VAMPIRE FINCH, THIS ANT LIKES TO DRINK BLOOD. IT'S WHOSE BLOOD IT DRINKS THAT MAKES IT CREEPIER.

We are Dracula ants. Our name might be frightening, but we won't hurt you. We have "claws" called <u>mandibles</u> that we snap, like you snap your fingers. This helps us catch prey as we cruise underground looking for Centipedes or termites.

We are kind of unusual as we don't eat the food we catch. We can't digest solid food. Instead, we bring the prey back and feed it to the larvae, baby ants.

So what do we do for food? We chew holes in the larvae and suck out their blood. Delectable! Believe it or not, this doesn't kill the larvae. The oddest thing is when we come around, the larvae try to flee and get away from us, but we have to eat, too!

One more thing. We are different from other ants in that we have abdomens that are similar to wasps. They may be our relatives.

38

Where do I live? ●

dracula ant and larvae

DID YOU KNOW?

- Hemolymph – blood in insects

- Non-destructive cannibalism is animals eating their own kind, but it does not kill them.

- Dracula ants are smaller than a grain of rice.

- Dracula ants can snap their mandibles at more than 200 miles per hour (90 meters a second), the fastest animal movement on record. It's 5,000 times quicker than the blink of an eye!

- Due to their wasp like waist, solid food would get stuck in their digestive tract and kill the ant, so they can only drink.

mandible

WE'RE GROSS, BUT
WE CAN'T HELP IT.
WE'RE FILTHY ANIMALS!

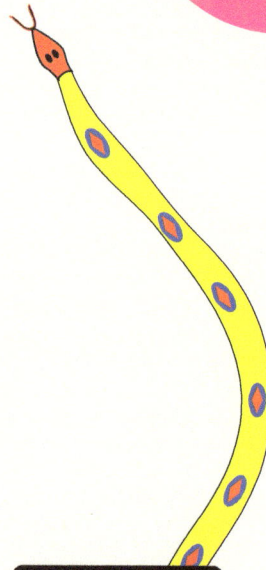

BUTT FIRST

VULTURES EAT DEAD ANIMALS FOUND IN THE WILD. VULTURES ARE LIKE GARBAGE MEN. IT'S NOT THE CLEANEST JOB, BUT SOMEONE HAS TO DO IT. WITHOUT VULTURES, THESE DEAD ANIMALS WOULD JUST LAY AROUND AND ROT. IT WOULD GET AWFULLY STINKY. IF YOU'VE EVER SEEN VULTURES IN BOOKS OR ON TELEVISION, THEY ALWAYS SEEM TO BE EATING VERY LARGE ANIMALS. THEIR BEAKS AREN'T THAT BIG TO BE ABLE TO TACKLE SUCH LARGE ANIMALS LIKE COWS, DEER, OR ELEPHANTS, SO HOW DO THEY DO IT? WAIT UNTIL YOU HEAR HOW VULTURES DIG INTO THE MEAT OF THESE LARGE ANIMALS.

41

Hey, can't you see I'm eating! Even though I have a sharp beak, it's not strong enough to cut through the skin of dead animals.

If large scavengers haven't torn away the skin yet, you won't believe what I have to do. I stick my head in the animal's butt! It's the softest part of the animal along with the eyeballs. Head first I go!

The animals I eat have died in the wild, and if it wasn't for me, the animal would rot and smell.

Do you notice my bare head and neck? That helps me stay cleaner after entering the animal butt first. It's like you putting your head into a bowl of spaghetti. It will stick to your hair, but if you were bald, the spaghetti would just slide off your head and you would stay clean, like me.

I don't get sick from eating rotten meat. I have a strong immune system, but you would get really sick, so don't eat rotten meat.

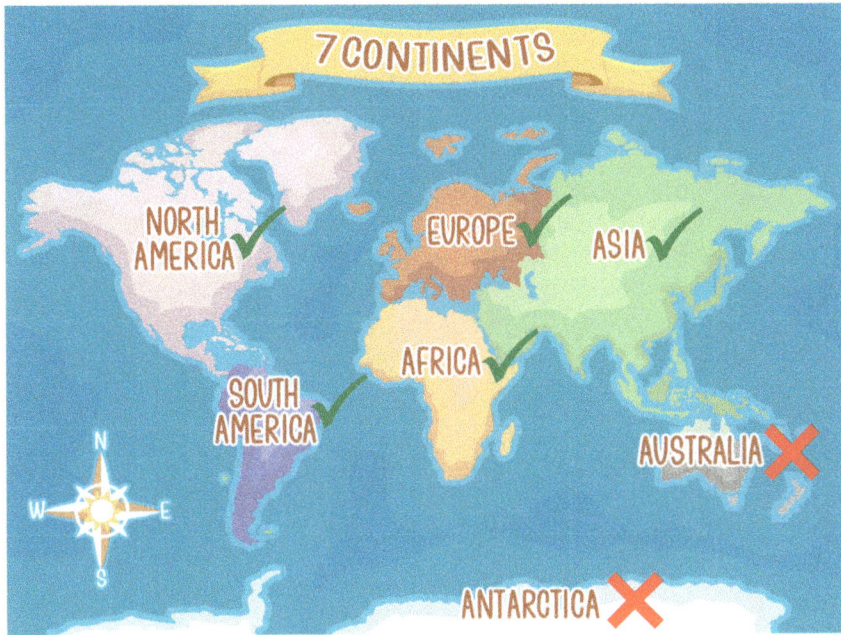

7 CONTINENTS

NORTH AMERICA ✓
EUROPE ✓
ASIA ✓
SOUTH AMERICA ✓
AFRICA ✓
AUSTRALIA ✗
ANTARCTICA ✗

Where do I live?

✓ Where I live

✗ Where I don't live

DID YOU KNOW?

- A vulture's beak is made of <u>keratin</u> (like human fingernails).

- Vultures defend themselves by throwing up.

- Many kinds of vultures can live in the wild for 25 years.

- Some vultures can fly as high as 35,000 feet (10,688 meters). That's how high a jet airplane flies.

- Vultures flap their wings as little as possible. They glide instead.

- Vultures are divided into two groups: New World (the Americas and Caribbean) and Old World (Europe, Asia, and Africa).

9 feet (2.7 meters)

bearded vulture

WE'RE GROSS, BUT WE CAN'T HELP IT. WE'RE FILTHY ANIMALS!

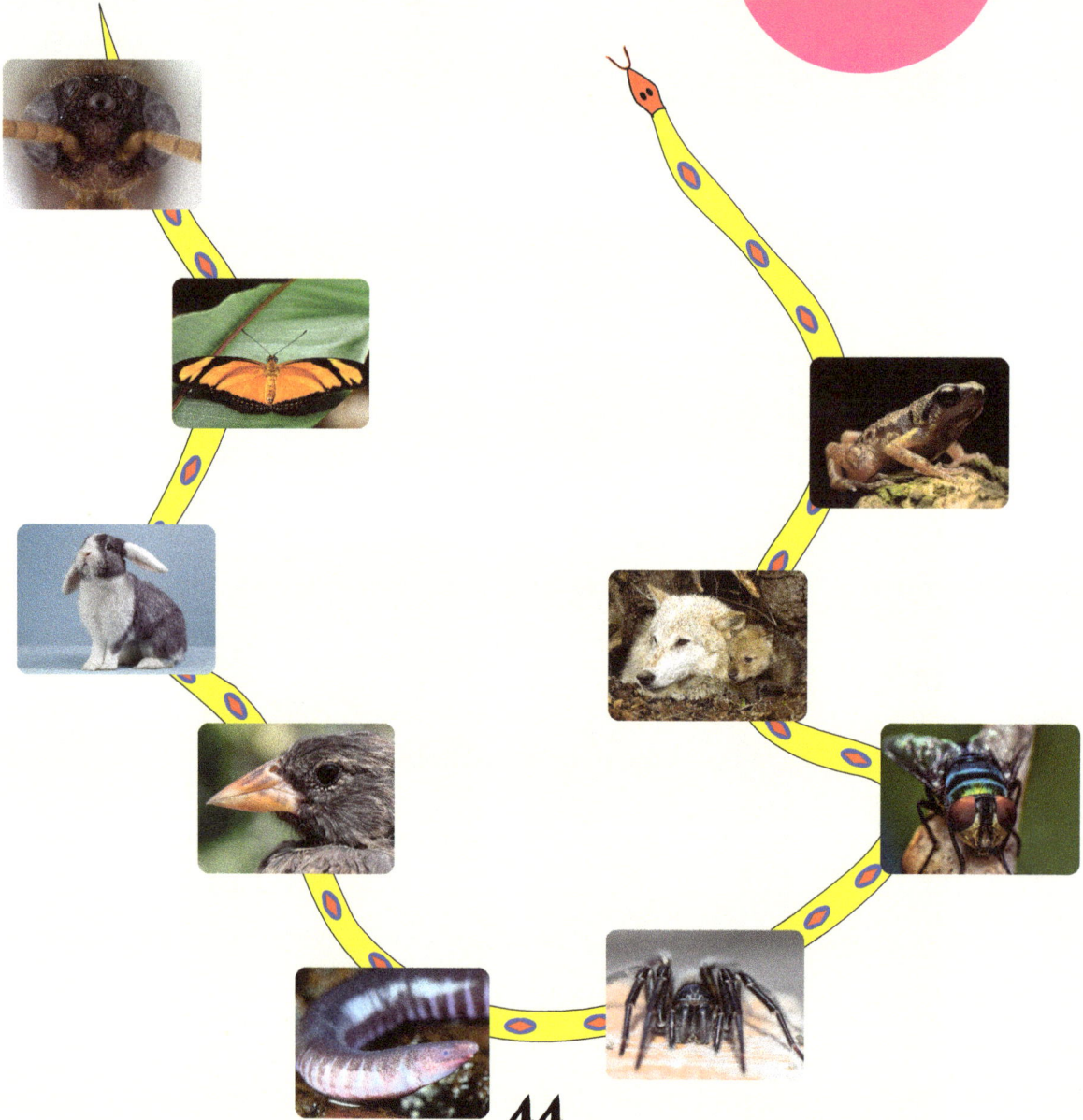

Bee Barf

SO, BY NOW YOU PROBABLY THINK ALL THESE CREATURES ARE PRETTY DARN FILTHY AND GROSS! WELL, WE THINK THAT SAME THING ABOUT YOU. WE FIGURE MANY OF YOU HAVE PROBABLY EATEN HONEY, RIGHT? MOST PEOPLE CAN'T PASS UP THE SWEET STUFF. WELL, IF YOU HAVE EATEN HONEY, YOU'VE EATEN BEE BARF! AND YOU THINK WE'RE GROSS?

Hi. I'm a honeybee. Right now I'm in my favorite spot doing my favorite thing, sucking nectar from the flower. I use nectar to make honey. If you have ever eaten honey, you'll want to pay attention to this.

When I drink nectar, I store it in a special place in my stomach that I call a "honey stomach" where it begins to turn into sugar.

When I return to the hive, I barf the nectar into another bee's mouth, and it goes into its honey stomach.

That bee barfs the liquid into another bee's mouth and goes into its honey stomach. This barfing continues from bee to bee until the nectar is all sugar.

The last bee barfs the watery honey liquid into honeycombs where it is stored. I live on it all winter.

Next time you eat honey, think about all the bee barf you're eating!

46

7 CONTINENTS

NORTH AMERICA

EUROPE

ASIA

AFRICA

SOUTH AMERICA

AUSTRALIA

ANTARCTICA

Where do I live?

The honeycomb is made from wax created by the bee's body. It is used to store larvae, honey, and pollen. You can eat the whole honeycomb, including the honey and waxy cells surrounding it. In addition, you can chew the waxy cells like gum.

DID YOU KNOW?

- There are three types of honeybees within a hive: the queen, the workers, and the drones.

- Honeybees have a proboscis just like the house fly.

- Honeybees dance to tell other bees where flowers are located.

- A colony can make 100 pounds of honey in one season.

- Buzzing is the sound of a bee's wings, which flap 230 times every minute.

- Some colonies have as many as 60,000 honeybees.

- A honeybee queen can lay 1,500 eggs per day.

- Honey is full of vitamins and minerals.

47

WE'RE GROSS, BUT WE CAN'T HELP IT. WE'RE FILTHY ANIMALS!

GLOSSARY

amphibian (am-FIB-ee-uhn): a cold-blooded animal that lives both on land and in water

cannibalism (CAN-nuh-buh-lih-zem): the eating of the flesh of an animal by an animal of the same kind

cecotropes (SEE-coh-tropes): soft feces that rabbits, hares, and other small mammals reingest to absorb additional nutrients

coprophagy (cu-PROHF-uh-jee): eating one's own poop

dermatotrophy (der-mat-uh-TROH-fee): to eat a parent's skin

dung (duhng): animal droppings or waste

feces (FEE-seez): food that is digested and pooped out; waste

hemolymph (HEE-muh-limf): blood in insects

immune system (ih-MUNE) (SIH-stum): organs and cells in living things that protect the body from illness and infection

keratin (KER-uh-tin): a protein that makes up fingernails, claws, horns, hoofs, etc.

lachryphagy (LAK-rihf-uh-jee): feeding on tears

matriphagy (mu-TRIHF-uh-jee): eating of the mother

massage (mah-SAJ): to rub parts of the body

mandible (MAN-duh-buhl): one of the front biting mouth parts in insects

nocturnal (naak-TUR-nuhl): active at night

proboscis (pro-BOS-kis): a long tube on the outside of the mouth of some insects used for sucking

regurgitate (ri-GUR-ji-teyt): to throw up or vomit

saliva (suh-LAHY-vuh): a liquid produced by glands in the mouth that helps us to chew and digest food

scavenger (SKA-vuyn-jur): an animal that finds and eats dead animals

tentacle (TEN-tuh-kuhl): a long thin body part on the head or mouth of some animals used for feeling or taking hold of things

PHOTO CREDITS